Stephanie Jeffs and Jacqui Thomas

Little EAGLE

Love from Amma Jean xxx 2005

WHO'S WHO IN THE BIBLE

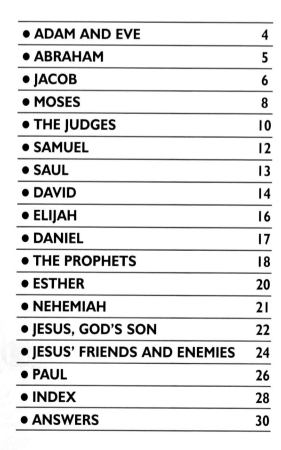

CONTENTS

Adam and Eve THE FIRST PEOPLE

Look it up

- God makes Adam and Eve GENESIS 2
- Adam and Eve disobey God GENESIS 3
- Cain and Abel GENESIS 4
- Noah and the flood GENESIS 6–8

Unique characteristics:

- The first people.
- Different from all the other creatures God created because they were able to think and speak, love, make choices and know God as their friend.
- The first to disobey God.

Occupations:

- Adam named all the animals God had made.
- Eve was Adam's special friend and partner.
- God asked them to look after the Garden of Eden, and to enjoy everything he had made.

Talents and strengths:

- Creative and imaginative, able to take care of the world God had made.

Special moment:

- In the beginning Adam walked and talked with God in the Garden of Eden and knew God as a special friend.

Greatest mistake:

- Eating the forbidden fruit from the tree of the knowledge of good and evil. God had told them clearly not to touch it, but they thought they knew better than God.

Greatest disappointments:

- Spoiling their friendship with God.
- Being forced to leave the Garden of Eden.

THEIR FAMILY

Cain *eldest son*

- Farmer.
- Was the first man to commit murder when he killed his brother, Abel.

Abel *second son*

- Shepherd.
- Gave God a gift that pleased him.
- Was murdered by his older brother.

Seth *third son*

- Born after Abel had died.

Seth's descendants

- The Bible traces the family line through Seth. It mentions **Enoch**, a man who loved God. The Bible says that he did not die, but was taken away by God. After him came **Methuselah**, Noah's grandfather. Said to be the oldest man who ever lived, he died aged 969.

The first people, Adam and Eve, lived in a beautiful garden called Eden.

GENESIS

Genesis, the first book in the Bible, tells us that God created a world full of good things and he was very pleased with it. Unfortunately, Adam and Eve disobeyed God, and were sent out of the Garden of Eden. Their son, Cain, was the first murderer. Later, Noah is described as 'the only good man' left in the world.

Noah

- The only man of his time who obeyed God.
- Was rescued by God from the flood which destroyed the world.
- Followed God's instructions and built an ark so that his family and the creatures God had made could escape the flood.
- God promised Noah and his descendants that he would never destroy the earth by flood again.
- Father of **Ham**, **Shem** and **Japheth**.

Connections

1) *Turn to page 7 to find someone like Abel, whose brothers planned to murder him.*

2) *God made Noah a promise. Find another promise God made on page 5.*

Abraham FATHER OF MANY NATIONS

Name:

● Abram, until God gave him the new name of Abraham, meaning 'father of many nations'.

Place of birth:

● The great city of Ur in Mesopotamia.

Where he lived:

● Canaan, the land promised him by God. It was a long way from Ur. Like many of the people in Canaan, Abraham and his family lived in tents and moved from place to place to find water and grass for his flocks.

Occupation:

● Wealthy nomad with many servants.

Outstanding characteristics:

● Listened to God.

● Trusted God and believed in God.

● Described as a 'friend of God'. When the high priest **Melchizedek**, king of Salem, met him he knew that Abraham had been chosen by God.

Major challenge:

● Despite many years of being childless, Abraham had the faith to believe God's promise of a son. Through that son he would have many descendants who would have a land of their own.

Weaknesses:

● Had trouble believing that his wife, Sarah, would have a baby in her old age, and so made Hagar his wife and became the father of Ishmael.

Most difficult experience:

● When God asked him to sacrifice his son, Isaac.

Happiest moment:

● When God stopped him from sacrificing his son.

HIS FAMILY

Terah *father*

● Lived in Ur and died in Haran.

● Also father to **Nahor** and **Haran**.

Sarah *wife*

● Exceptionally beautiful.

● Was unable to have children until she gave birth to Isaac in her old age.

● Offered Abraham her slave girl, Hagar, to be his second wife, but regretted it when Hagar's son, Ishmael, was born.

ABRAHAM'S FAITH

Abraham's ancestors worshipped many gods, but Abraham believed in the 'one God' who promised to make him 'father of many nations'. The rest of the Bible story shows how this was worked out in history, starting with the Hebrew people.

God told Abraham that he would have many descendants: 'as many as the stars in the sky'.

Isaac *son*

● He later became the father of Esau and Jacob.

Ishmael *son*

● Only son of Abraham and Hagar.

● God promised that his descendants would also become a nation.

Lot *nephew*

● Went with Abraham to Canaan.

● Wanted the best land for himself.

● Eventually settled near the evil city of Sodom, and was rescued by two angels when the city was destroyed by God.

HIS SERVANTS

Hagar *Sarah's slave girl*

● Egyptian mother of Abraham's first child, Ishmael.

● Ran away from home, with Ishmael, because of Sarah's unkindness.

● Met an angel who told her that God would look after her son.

Eliezer *Abraham's servant*

● Abraham's chief servant and adopted heir before the birth of Ishmael.

Look it up

- *Abraham leaves for Canaan and receives God's promise* GENESIS 12:1–7
- *God promises Abraham a son* GENESIS 15:1–6; 18:1–15; 21:1–7
- *Hagar and Ishmael* GENESIS 16:1–16
- *Abraham prepares to sacrifice Isaac* GENESIS 22:1–19

Connections

1) Turn to page 23 to find another couple promised a son by God, despite their old age.

2) Abraham's descendants were promised the land of Canaan. Find two other places they lived in on pages 7 and 17.

3) Read how another couple were told by an angel that they would have a special son on page 23.

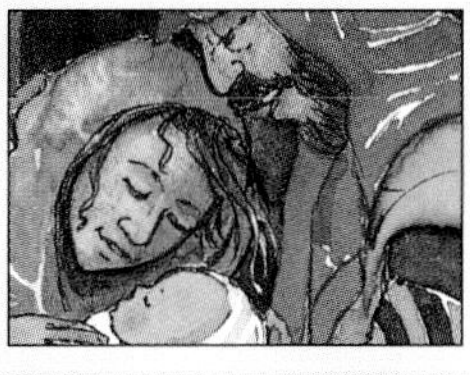

GOD'S PLANS

The stories of Jacob and his sons show that God can use all sorts of people in his plans. Jacob was persuaded by his mother to pretend that he was Esau so that he could inherit the elder son's share of money and possessions from his father Isaac. When Jacob himself became a father he unwisely showed that he loved Joseph more than the others and made his other sons jealous. Yet God met with Jacob and promised to 'bless the earth' through his descendants. King David and, much later, Jesus Christ, were both descended from Judah, one of Jacob's sons.

Jacob THE MAN WHO WRESTLED WITH GOD

Jacob was the father of twelve sons and one daughter.

Occupation:

- Shepherd and livestock owner.
- Father of a huge family.

Where he lived:

- Canaan and Egypt.

By building up big flocks of spotted sheep, Jacob became rich.

Esau was a hunter; Jacob offered him some stew in return for his 'birthright'.

Childhood:

- Held on to his twin brother Esau's foot when he was born.
- Youngest twin and the child his mother loved best.
- Enjoyed staying at home while his brother went hunting.
- Gave his starving brother food in return for the right to be head of the family.

Main characteristics:

- Determined to get what he wanted.

Faults:

- Deceitful: he tricked his brother and deceived his father.
- Later in life, he showed that he loved Joseph more than his other children and upset his other sons.

Frustrations:

- He ran away from his home and family because he was afraid of Esau's anger.
- His uncle Laban deceived him, and he married Leah instead of Rachel.

Important moments:

- When God changed his name from Jacob, which means 'deceiver', to Israel, which means 'God struggles', following the time when Jacob wrestled with God's angel.
- When he met Esau for the first time after he had run away from home, and despite his fears, was greeted with a hug.
- Adopted Joseph's two sons as his own. Later their families were given land in Canaan like the families of Jacob's own children.

Major achievements:

- Found out how to breed better sheep than his uncle Laban and so made himself rich.
- The descendants of his twelve sons became the twelve tribes of Israel.
- Sometimes the prophets in the Bible called the nation of Israel 'Jacob' when they spoke of God's love for his people.

Great experiences:

- Had a dream in which he saw a ladder leading up to heaven, and God promised to be with him and all his descendants.
- Wrestled with God's angel, and refused to let go, until God had blessed him.

Great sadnesses:

- His wife Rachel's death in childbirth.
- When he thought that his son Joseph had been killed by a wild animal.

Biggest surprise:

- The discovery that Joseph was not dead, but was governor of Egypt.

After deceiving both his father and his brother, Jacob fled to Mesopotamia.

Leah would have been veiled at the wedding feast, so Jacob was tricked into taking her as his wife.

HIS FAMILY

Isaac *father*

- Abraham and Sarah's promised son.
- Half-brother of Ishmael.
- Married Rebekah.

Rebekah *mother*

- Daughter of **Bethuel**, son of **Nahor** and **Milcah**, Abraham's brother and his wife.
- Found as a wife for Isaac by Abraham's servant from among his own family in Mesopotamia.
- Drew water from the well and gave it to Abraham's servant, and then drew water again for his camels.

Esau *brother*

- The eldest twin son of Isaac and Rebekah, and the son Isaac loved best.
- Tricked twice by Jacob out of receiving his father's blessing.
- Forgave Jacob in later life.

Laban *uncle*

- Father of Leah and Rachel.
- Made Jacob work for seven years before he could marry Rachel.
- Tricked Jacob into marrying Leah, and then into working for another seven years without pay for Rachel.

HIS WIVES AND CHILDREN

Leah

- Rachel's older sister and Jacob's first wife.
- Mother to six sons – **Reuben**, **Simeon**, **Levi**, **Judah**, **Issachar** and **Zebulun**, and one daughter, **Dinah**.

Rachel

- Waited seven years to marry Jacob.
- Tricked out of being Jacob's first wife by her father, Laban.
- Unable to have children for many years, she eventually had two sons, **Joseph** and **Benjamin**.

Zilpah *Leah's servant*

- Mother of **Gad** and **Asher**.

Bilhah *Rachel's servant*

- Mother of **Dan** and **Naphtali**.

Joseph

- Jacob's much-loved son.
- Rachel's first son.
- Given a special coat by his father.
- His jealous brothers plotted to kill him, but threw him into a pit and later sold him into slavery instead.
- Taken to Egypt, where he served **Potiphar**, a captain in the Egyptian guard.
- Was put in prison, where he stayed for years until it was found that God had given him the ability to understand dreams.
- Became governor of Egypt after explaining pharaoh's dreams.
- Married **Asenath**, daughter of the priest, **Potiphera**.
- Was eventually reunited with his family who came to live with him in Egypt during a famine.
- Had two sons, **Manasseh** and **Ephraim**, who were adopted by Jacob.

Look it up

- *Jacob and Esau are born* GENESIS 25:24–28
- *Esau 'sells' his birthright to Jacob* GENESIS 25:29–34
- *Jacob tricks his father* GENESIS 27:1–29
- *Jacob's dream* GENESIS 28:10–22
- *Jacob wrestles with God* GENESIS 32:22–32
- *Joseph's brothers trick Jacob* GENESIS 37:21–32
- *Joseph meets his brothers again* GENESIS 45:1–28

Connections

1) Find on page 9 the name of one of Levi's descendants who was the first high priest in the Bible.

2) Turn to page 9 to see when Jacob's family returned to Canaan.

3) Look at pages 22 and 23 to see why some other men called Joseph and Simeon were important in Jesus' life story.

4) Find three other men whose names were changed on pages 5, 24 and 26.

When Jacob gave a special coat to his favourite son, Joseph, his other sons were jealous and angry. Later they plotted to kill Joseph.

Moses

THE MAN WHO MET GOD FACE TO FACE

Moses and his brother Aaron pleaded with the pharaoh to free the Israelites from slavery.

A HOME IN EGYPT

The Israelites had been in Egypt for 400 years, first as welcome visitors but later as slaves, building palaces and big cities for the Egyptian kings or pharaohs.

THE TEN COMMANDMENTS

God gave these laws to help people live good lives. God told them they should worship only him, not idols made of wood and stone. He told them how to respect each other, summed up by Jesus as loving God with all your heart, mind and strength; and treating others as you would like them to treat you.

Occupations:

- Prince, then shepherd, then a great leader of God's people.

Education:

- Brought up in Egypt, where God's people, the Israelites, were slaves, by an Egyptian princess.

Childhood:

- Escaped death as a baby when his mother hid him in a basket along the bank of the River Nile.
- Found by the pharaoh's daughter, who brought him up as her own son.

Major achievements:

- Chosen by God to take all the Israelites from Egypt to the Promised Land.
- Talked to God, and was given God's laws for his people on Mount Sinai.

Major challenge:

- Persuading the pharaoh, the king of Egypt, to let the Israelites leave Egypt. God used Moses to turn the water of the River Nile into blood, sent a plague of locusts, frogs and flies, created a massive hailstorm, and caused all the animals to die. The pharaoh still refused to let the Israelites leave Egypt.

Most memorable night:

- When God protected all the Israelites while the firstborn sons of all the Egyptians died. Then the pharaoh ordered the Israelites out of Egypt.

Mistakes:

- Killed an Egyptian slave-driver when he saw him beating an Israelite slave.
- Argued with God in Egypt, and made excuses not to be the Israelites' leader.
- Disobeyed God in the desert on the way to the Promised Land.

Frustrations:

- The pharaoh kept changing his mind, first agreeing to let the Israelites leave Egypt, then refusing.
- After the Israelites had left Egypt, they grumbled and moaned about their living conditions. Some even said they wished they were back in Egypt!
- The journey to the Promised Land should have taken only a few months, but the people refused to trust God, so they lived for forty years in the desert.

Disappointments:

- Unable to enter the Promised Land, because of his disobedience to God.

Great experiences:

- Heard God speak to him from the middle of a bush which was on fire, but did not burn up.
- Held out his hand, and saw God separate the waters of the Red Sea so that he could lead the Israelites to the other side and safety.
- Saw God provide food and water for his people while living in the desert.
- Received God's laws on behalf of his people and saw God's glory pass by while he hid in a cleft in a rock.

When Moses came down from Mount Sinai he was furious because the people had made a golden calf and were worshipping it.

HIS FAMILY

Jochebed

● Wife of Amran.

● Saved Moses when pharaoh ordered all baby boys to be killed.

Aaron *brother*

● Helped Moses ask the pharaoh to let the Israelites go.

● In the desert, encouraged the people to worship a golden calf instead of worshipping God.

● Descended from Levi, later became the first high priest.

● Disobeyed God, and was therefore forbidden to enter the Promised Land.

Miriam *sister*

● Watched as baby Moses was hidden by the River Nile.

● When Moses had led the Israelites across the Red Sea to safety Miriam sang and danced in praise to God and all the women did the same.

● Later Miriam rebelled against Moses, and was punished by God.

Jethro *father-in-law*

● Gave Moses a home and a job as a shepherd after he had murdered an Egyptian.

● After the Israelites had left Egypt, he advised Moses to share his workload with other leaders.

Thousands of Israelite slaves fled from Egypt by night, taking everything with them.

Zipporah *wife*

● Met Moses when she and her sisters were trying to get water from a well.

Gershom and Eliezer *sons*

HIS FRIENDS AND SUPPORTERS

Joshua

● After Moses' death, he led the Israelites over the River Jordan into the Promised Land.

● Sent out as a spy into Canaan, he was one of only two Israelites born in Egypt to enter the Promised Land forty years later.

Caleb

● One of the twelve men sent by Moses to spy out the Promised Land of Canaan.

● Only he and Joshua trusted that God would look after them.

● He entered Canaan forty years later.

Hur

● One of Moses' supporters and, with Aaron, his deputy.

Bezalel

● Chosen by God to design God's meeting place, the tabernacle.

TROUBLEMAKERS

The Israelite people

● Spent most of their time on the journey from Egypt complaining, refusing to do what Moses said, and disobeying God.

Abihu and Nadab

● Moses' nephews.

● Chosen as priests, they ignored God's instructions.

Korah, Abiram and Dathan

● Tried to challenge Moses' leadership.

God's first law was 'You shall not worship any other gods but me'.

Look it up

- *Moses the baby is saved from death* EXODUS 2:1–10
- *God speaks to Moses from a burning bush* EXODUS 3:1–10
- *The plagues of Egypt* EXODUS 7:14 – 11:10
- *God 'passes over' the Israelites* EXODUS 12
- *Moses leads the Israelites across the Red Sea* EXODUS 14:5–31
- *The Ten Commandments* EXODUS 20
- *The golden calf* EXODUS 32
- *The spies enter Canaan (the Promised Land)* NUMBERS 13:1–2, 23–33

Connections

1) Turn to page 5 to find out where the name the 'Promised Land' came from.

2) Read how the Israelites came to be living in Egypt on page 7.

3) Find which prophet God provided with food and water in a famine on page 16.

4) Moses' brother and sister did not always support him. Find out what Jesus' brothers thought about him on page 23.

5) Discover who else was a shepherd before they became a leader of God's people on page 14.

Deborah was a prophet. She listened to God and passed on his message to the people.

The Judges GOD'S CHOSEN LEADERS

NAME: DEBORAH

Occupation:

- Prophet, fourth and only female judge, leader for forty years.

Disappointments:

- Deborah asked Barak to raise an army to fight King Jabin, and he refused to go without her.

Greatest achievement:

- Successfully led the Israelite army against King Jabin and his commander, Sisera.

Greatest celebration:

- When victorious, Deborah and Barak sang a song of praise to God.

DEBORAH'S FAMILY

Lappidoth ***husband***

HER ENEMIES

Jabin ***king of Hazor***

- Cruelly oppressed the Israelites for twenty years.

Sisera

- Commander of Jabin's army, who was killed by Jael.

HER SUPPORTERS

Barak

- Chosen by God to lead the Israelite army.
- Did not believe God would give them victory and refused to go into battle without Deborah.

Jael

- Married to **Heber**, an ally of King Jabin.
- Offered Sisera a hiding place in her tent, and killed him by hammering a tent peg through his head.

Jael killed Sisera, the leader of the enemy army, with a tent peg.

NAME: GIDEON

Occupation:

- Farmer, soldier and Israel's fifth judge.

Major achievements:

- Obeyed God and led the Israelite army, despite his fear.
- Led the Israelites to victory over the Midianites.

Weaknesses:

- Was afraid to obey God's instructions until God proved himself with a woollen fleece.
- Kept Midianite gold, which was used for the worship of idols.
- Failed to discipline his son, Abimelech.

GIDEON'S FAMILY

Joash ***father***

Abimelech ***son***

- Wanted to be a ruler like Gideon.
- Killed all but one of his seventy brothers.
- Attacked one town, but was fatally injured when a woman hurled part of a millstone from the top of the tower, hitting Abimelech on the head.

Jotham ***son***

- Only surviving brother to escape Abimelech's murder attack.
- Warned the people of Shechem not to make Abimelech king.

When Gideon's army of just 300 men beat the Midianites, they knew that God had saved them.

WARS AND LAWS

Joshua had taken God's people into Canaan, the Promised Land. One by one the cities of Canaan had been conquered, and each of the twelve tribes of Israel had settled in its own area. But it was a time of fighting and wars as there were still Canaanite tribes living in the land.

After Joshua's death God's people started to live like the tribes around them, worshipping idols made of wood and stone, and forgetting God's laws. God used the judges to remind his people to follow him by keeping his laws. The judges were also appointed to help fight their enemies.

NAME: SAMSON

Occupation:

Israel's twelfth judge.

Childhood:

- His parents were told by an angel that they would have a son who would save God's people from their enemy, the Philistines.

Special characteristics:

A Nazirite, chosen by God to serve him and save Israel from the Philistines.

- Wore his hair in seven braids and never had it cut.

Grew to be superhumanly strong and powerful.

Samson was so strong he was able to tear apart a lion with his bare hands.

Major achievements:

- Led Israel for twenty years.
- Killed 1,000 men with the jaw bone of a donkey.
- Brought down the Philistine temple killing himself and more than 3,000 Philistines.

Greatest mistakes:

- Disobeyed God and told Delilah the secret of his strength.

Greatest humiliation:

- Losing his strength, being blinded and taken prisoner by the Philistines.

SAMSON'S FAMILY

Manoah ***father***

- He and his wife were unable to have children until an angel told them they would have a son.

Samson asked God to give him back his strength so he could pull down the temple on himself and his enemies.

- Accepted God's will for them and brought up Samson to serve God.

HIS ENEMIES

The Philistines

- A constant enemy of all the Israelites, occupying the land nearby.

Delilah

- Pretended to love Samson while paid by the Philistines to find the secret of his strength.
- Cut Samson's hair so that his strength would leave him.

OTHER JUDGES

Othniel

- Israel's first judge and Caleb's nephew.
- Led Israel to victory against the Arameans.
- Judged Israel for forty years.

Ehud

- Rescued Israel from **Eglon**, king of Moab, by killing him.
- Judged Israel for eighty years.

Jephthah

- Saved Israel from the Ammonites.
- Promised God that if he beat them he would sacrifice the first thing he saw when he returned to his house: it was his daughter. He kept his promise to God.

Gideon's only 'weapons' were a flaming torch and a ram's horn trumpet.

Look it up

- *Deborah leads the Israelites* JUDGES 4
- *Death of Sisera* JUDGES 4:17–21
- *God speaks to Gideon* JUDGES 6:11–24
- *The woollen fleece* JUDGES 6:36–40
- *Gideon fights the Midianites* JUDGES 7
- *Samson kills a lion* JUDGES 14:5–9
- *Samson and Delilah* JUDGES 16:4–21
- *Samson's last prayer* JUDGES 16:23–31

It was at a great sacrifice to the Philistine god Dagon that Samson gained his last victory.

Connections

1) Read on page 14 about another man who helped defeat a Philistine.

2) Ehud helped Israel defeat the Moabites. Look on page 14 for the ancestor of King David and Jesus who was also a Moabite.

3) Deborah led the Israelites into victory. Turn to page 20 to find another woman who helped rescue God's people.

4) Delilah betrayed Samson to the Philistines. Find out who betrayed Jesus on page 24.

Samuel THE BOY WHO HEARD GOD'S VOICE

Look it up

- *Hannah prays for a baby* *I SAMUEL 1:9–20*
- *God speaks to Samuel* *I SAMUEL 3:1–21*
- *The death of Eli* *I SAMUEL 4:12–18*

Connections

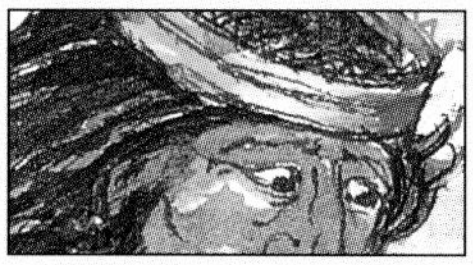

1) Read page 14 to find another man like Eli who failed to discipline his sons.

2) Look for other women without children in the Bible whose prayers were answered by God on pages 5, 7, 11 and 23.

3) Turn to page 9 to find a priest who set a bad example to the people.

THE COVENANT BOX

The laws God gave Moses on Mount Sinai were carved on stone and kept in a gold-covered box so holy that no one was allowed to touch it. Also called the Ark of the Covenant, wherever God's people went, the box went too, carried on two poles, as a sign of God's presence with them.

Occupations:

● Last of Israel's judges, prophet and priest.

Education:

● Trained to serve God in the Temple at Shiloh.

Childhood:

● Cared for and taught by Eli, the priest.

● Received a visit and a new coat from his mother each year.

● Heard God calling his name.

● Received a warning from God to Eli about his disobedient family.

Major achievements:

● Led Israel for many years, a good and wise judge.

● Anointed and advised Israel's first two kings, King Saul and King David.

● Remained faithful to God throughout his life.

Disappointments:

● God's people rejected his leadership, preferring a king.

● Saul, the first king he anointed, disobeyed God.

As a young boy, Samuel lived at the Temple in Shiloh. His mother brought him a new coat each year.

● Samuel's children did not serve God faithfully.

HIS FAMILY

Elkanah *father*

● Husband of Peninnah and Hannah.

Hannah *mother*

● Loved most by Elkanah, her husband, but childless for many years.

● Prayed for a son and promised to give him back to God to serve him in the Temple.

● Had five more children.

Peninnah

● Elkanah's other wife.

● Unkind to Hannah because she was childless.

Joel and Abijah *sons*

● Appointed as judges by their father but rejected because of their dishonesty.

HIS TEACHER

Eli

● High priest at the Temple at Shiloh, he saw Hannah praying.

● Brought up Samuel to serve God.

● Failed to discipline his own two sons.

● Died when he heard that the special Covenant Box had been captured by the Philistines.

Hophni and Phinehas

● Eli's sons.

● Killed in battle when the Covenant Box was captured.

One night, while the boy Samuel was sleeping, God spoke to him. This was a sign that God had chosen Samuel to be his servant.

Saul ISRAEL'S FIRST KING

The Israelites wanted a king to lead them in battle, like the nations around them. Saul was the first of these kings.

Occupation:
- King and military leader.

Childhood:
- Born when Israel was ruled by the prophet Samuel, the last of the judges.
- Was anointed king by Samuel secretly.

Outstanding features:
- Tall, strong, healthy and handsome.
- As a young man, humble and wanting to follow God.
- A good soldier.

His weaknesses:
- Suffered from bad moods and depression which were helped at first by David's harp-playing.
- Became jealous of David after he defeated Goliath which made him angry and dangerous.

His downfall:
- Became selfish and did not obey God.
- Would not take Samuel's advice.
- Lost the respect of his people.
- Lost God's blessing as king.

HIS FAMILY

Kish ***father***
- A wealthy landowner.

Jonathan ***son***
- He was David's best friend, and warned David when Saul wanted to kill him.
- A brave soldier and a skilled archer.
- Father of **Mephibosheth**.

David the shepherd boy soothed King Saul's angry words by playing the harp.

Michal ***daughter***
- Married to David which made Saul jealous.
- Helped David escape from Saul.

Ish-Bosheth ***son***
- Survived Jonathan, so was proclaimed a rival king to David after Saul's death.

HIS SUPPORTER

Abner
- Commander of King Saul's army, he eventually changed sides and supported David.

HIS ENEMY

Goliath
- A Philistine giant, 3.2 metres tall, who challenged Saul and his army.
- As a Philistine, he was one of the groups of people fighting the Israelites for the land of Canaan.
- Killed by the young David, the only one brave enough to fight him.

Look it up

- *The Israelites ask for a king* I SAMUEL 8:4–22
- *Samuel anoints Saul* I SAMUEL 9:1 – 10:24
- *David plays the harp for Saul* I SAMUEL 16:14–23
- *The death of Saul* I SAMUEL 31:1–13

Connections

1) Turn to page 14 to find out how Goliath was killed.

2) The prophet Jeremiah announced that God would send a new king. Find out who he would be descended from on page 19.

3) Find out on page 26 about another man named Saul who changed his name.

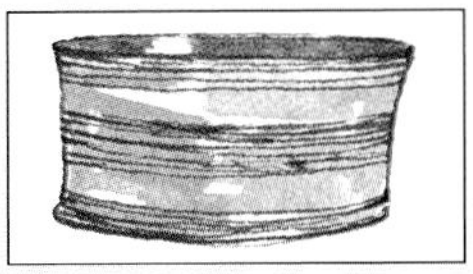

ANOINTING A KING

When the people of Israel asked Samuel for a king, so that they could be just like the other people who lived around them, Samuel told them it would lead to trouble because God was their king. When they insisted, God led Samuel to anoint Saul. Samuel poured some special olive oil on Saul's head as a sign that God had chosen him. It was up to Saul to live in a way that pleased God.

David THE SHEPHERD BOY WHO BECAME A KING

David was only a young shepherd boy when he was secretly anointed next king of Israel by the prophet Samuel.

David defended his father's sheep by killing lions and bears with his shepherd's sling.

David used his shepherd's sling and a small stone to kill Goliath the giant.

Ruth, a Moabite woman, was David's great grandmother. She followed Naomi to Bethlehem where Boaz married her.

Occupations:
● Shepherd, soldier, king.

Childhood:
● Youngest of eight sons, his three eldest brothers, **Eliab**, **Abinadab** and **Shammah**, had followed King Saul to war.

● Brought up on the family farm outside Bethlehem.

Outstanding abilities:
● A good shot with a shepherd's sling, killing lions and bears while looking after his father's sheep.

● A skilled harpist, playing for King Saul.

● A poet, writing many of the psalms in the Bible.

● A keen soldier, one of Saul's generals, and when outlawed, was able to outwit Saul's attempt to capture him.

● A wise administrator who governed Israel well.

Great experiences:
● Was anointed Israel's second king by the prophet Samuel.

● Brought God's Covenant Box back to Jerusalem, and led the people in worshipping God.

Frustrations:
● His relationship with King Saul, who tried to kill him.

Major achievements:
● Killed Goliath with a stone and a shepherd's sling.

● He led many great military campaigns against Israel's enemies.

● Established Israel as a powerful nation and remained loyal to God throughout his life.

Serious failings:
● Arranged **Uriah**'s murder so he could marry Bathsheba, Uriah's wife.

● Failed to discipline his children.

Disappointments:
● Betrayed by some of his friends and children.

Great sadnesses:
● The death of his best friend, Jonathan.

● The betrayal and death of his son, Absalom.

HIS FAMILY

Jesse *father*
● Son of **Obed**.

Boaz *great grandfather*
● Son of **Salmon**.

● Relative of **Elimelech** who married **Naomi** and had two sons, **Mahlon** and **Kilion**, and moved to Moab when there was famine in Bethlehem.

● Owned the field where Mahlon's Moabite wife, **Ruth**, came to pick up leftover grain after her husband had died.

● Married Ruth and had a son, Obed.

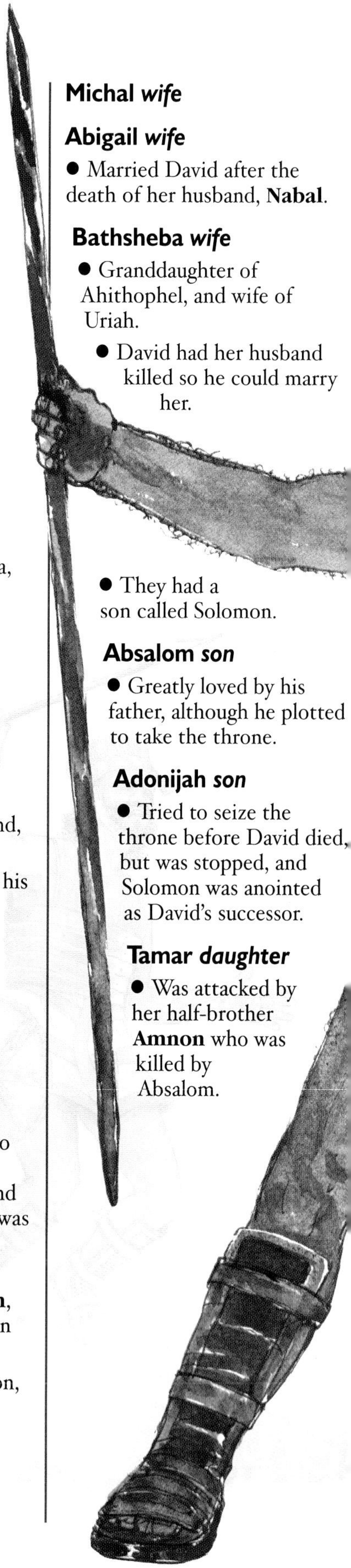

Michal *wife*

Abigail *wife*
● Married David after the death of her husband, **Nabal**.

Bathsheba *wife*
● Granddaughter of Ahithophel, and wife of Uriah.

● David had her husband killed so he could marry her.

● They had a son called Solomon.

Absalom *son*
● Greatly loved by his father, although he plotted to take the throne.

Adonijah *son*
● Tried to seize the throne before David died, but was stopped, and Solomon was anointed as David's successor.

Tamar *daughter*
● Was attacked by her half-brother **Amnon** who was killed by Absalom.

King Saul offered David his sword and armour to fight Goliath. But it was too big and heavy for the young David.

David's son, Solomon, Israel's richest and wisest king, built a Temple in Jerusalem.

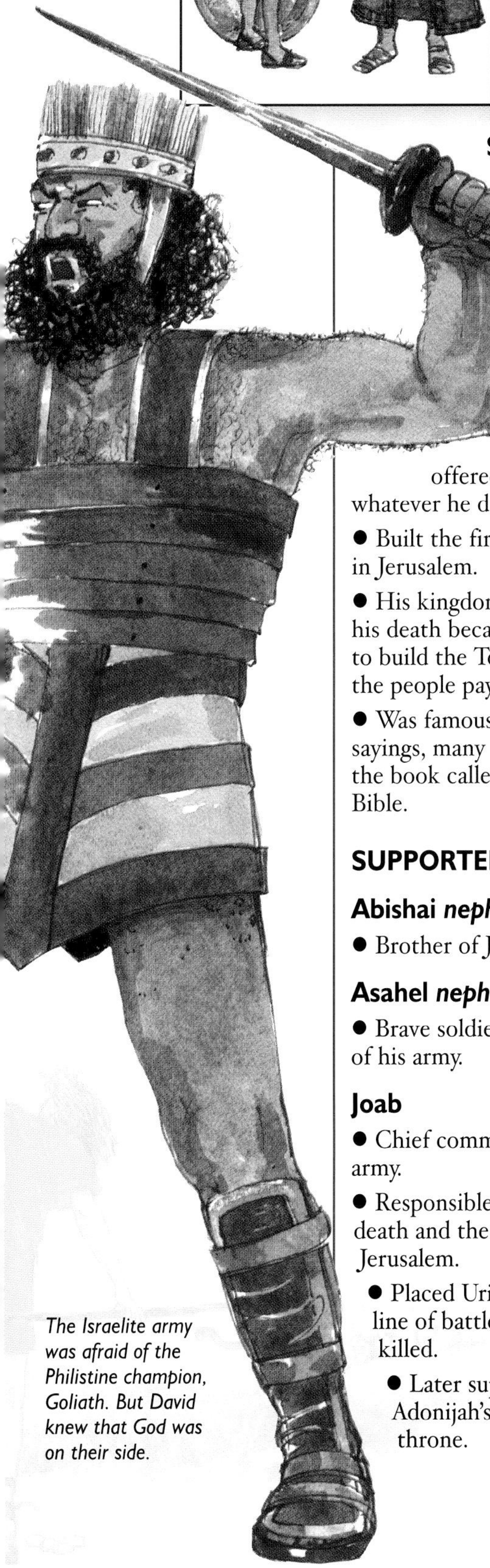

The Israelite army was afraid of the Philistine champion, Goliath. But David knew that God was on their side.

Solomon *son*

- Son of David and Bathsheba.
- Became a rich and powerful king.
- He chose wisdom when God offered to give him whatever he desired.
- Built the first Temple to God in Jerusalem.
- His kingdom broke up after his death because he used slaves to build the Temple and made the people pay heavy taxes.
- Was famous for his wise sayings, many to be found in the book called Proverbs in the Bible.

SUPPORTERS

Abishai *nephew*

- Brother of Joab.

Asahel *nephew*

- Brave soldier and commander of his army.

Joab

- Chief commander of David's army.
- Responsible for **Abner**'s death and the capture of Jerusalem.
- Placed Uriah in the front line of battle so he would be killed.
- Later supported Adonijah's claim to the throne.

Hushai

- Acted as David's spy.

Benaiah

- Captain of David's bodyguard, a valiant fighter, who had killed a lion.
- Helped make Solomon king.

FRIENDS

Jonathan *King Saul's son*

Ahimelech

- Head priest at Nob, killed by Saul.

Nathan

- A prophet, and David's adviser.
- He made David realise that he was wrong to arrange Uriah's death.
- Also reminded him of God's forgiveness to people who are truly sorry.

TRAITORS

Abiathar

- Escaped Saul's attempts to murder his family, joined David and became one of his advisers.
- Plotted against David, and supported Adonijah who wanted to be king.

Ahithophel

- A trusted friend to David, who became a conspirator with Absalom.

Look it up

- *The Covenant Box comes back to Jerusalem*
  I Samuel 6:10–19
- *David is anointed king of Israel by Samuel*
  I Samuel 16:1–13
- *David kills Goliath*
  I Samuel 17
- *David and Bathsheba*
  2 Samuel 11
- *Nathan and David*
  2 Samuel 12:1–10

CONSEQUENCES

Although David was very special to God, he committed serious sins. He knew God could forgive him (see Psalm 51 in the Bible) but the things he had done wrong did affect him in later life: his children argued with him and with each other, and some of his friends betrayed him.

Connections

1) Find which judge on page 11 killed a lion with his bare hands.

2) See page 12 to find out who died when he heard that the Philistines had stolen the precious Covenant Box.

3) David made Jerusalem the capital city and his son King Solomon built a fantastic Temple there. Turn to page 18 to find out what happened to the great city of Jerusalem in 586 BCE.

Elijah THE MAN WHO SPOKE OUT FOR GOD

Look it up

- *God takes care of Elijah* 1 KINGS 17:1–6
- *The widow of Zarephath* 1 KINGS 17:7–24
- *Elijah escapes from Jezebel* 1 KINGS 19:3–9
- *Elisha is chosen* 1 KINGS 19:19–21
- *Naaman is healed* 2 KINGS 5:1–14

Connections

1) Find someone else on page 4 who, like Elijah, did not die, but was taken up to heaven.

2) Turn to page 8 to find out about the commandments that King Ahab and Queen Jezebel did not follow.

3) Elijah and Elisha both spoke out against the worship of other gods. Look for others who have spoken out against the same thing on pages 18 and 19.

IDOL WORSHIP

As God's people, the Israelites, were different from the many nations around them. They were to worship and obey God, whose first law was 'worship no God but me'. But again and again, God's people turned away from him and started to worship idols. These were often statues made of wood, metal or stone, and people believed that these 'gods' controlled the weather, affected fertility or brought good luck.

Occupation:

- Prophet.

His message:

- Elijah told King Ahab that it was wrong to worship false gods and idols: God's people were to worship the one true God and obey his laws.

On Mount Carmel, Elijah challenged the prophets of Baal to decide whose God was the one true God and then follow him.

God sent Elijah to King Ahab to warn him to turn away from idol worship.

Major achievements:

- Stood up to King Ahab and his wife Jezebel, and made them angry.
- Spoke up for God against the prophets of the false god, Baal.
- Predicted the beginning and end of a three-year drought which caused a terrible famine.

Great experiences:

- Was looked after by God and given food by ravens, then by the **widow of Zarephath**, whose supplies of oil and flour never ran out during the famine.
- When the widow's son died, Elijah prayed to God and the boy came back to life.
- Saw God send down fire from heaven to burn the sacrifice he had made.
- Heard God speaking to him.
- Was taken up to heaven in a chariot of fire, drawn by horses of fire, in the middle of a whirlwind.

Most frightening moment:

- When Queen Jezebel threatened to kill him, and he ran away into hiding.

HIS ENEMIES

Ahab

- Son of **Omri**, he was the most evil king of Israel.
- Married to Jezebel, he allowed her to build a temple to the false god, Baal, in the palace.
- Fatally wounded in battle.
- Ahab's son, **Ahaziah**, became king after him.

Jezebel

- From the city of Tyre, a forceful, strong-willed woman who married King Ahab.
- Worshipped the false god Baal and the fertility goddess Ashtoreth, and supported 450 priests.
- Arranged **Naboth**'s death because he would not sell Ahab his vineyard.
- Mother of **Athaliah**, who married **Jehoram**, king of Judah, and became a powerful queen mother by killing all the members of the royal family except **Prince Joash**, who escaped.
- Eventually died a gruesome death.

HIS FOLLOWERS

Elisha *son of Shaphat*

- Left his family to follow Elijah.
- Ordered the anointing of **Jehu**, son of **Jehoshaphat**, who then killed **King Joram**, son of Ahab and Jezebel, and all the surviving members of their family and their close friends.
- Performed miracles to help those in need, including healing **Naaman**'s leprosy.

Obadiah *palace official*

- Although Elijah didn't know it, Obadiah risked his own life by secretly protecting 100 of God's prophets from Jezebel's murderous intentions.

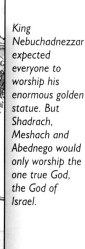

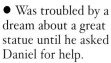

Daniel GOD'S FOLLOWER IN A FOREIGN LAND

Name:

● Daniel, until he was trained for the king's service, when he was renamed **Belteshazzar**.

Occupation:

● A Jewish captive in Babylon who became the adviser of kings.

Where he lived:

● Probably born in Judah, but taken to Babylon when young.

Education:

● Specially chosen to learn the Babylonian language and literature.

● Trained for three years to serve the king.

Personal qualities:

● Remained faithful to God in a foreign country.

● Brave, intelligent and quick to learn.

● Able to interpret dreams and visions, with God's help.

Major achievements:

● Was a well-respected adviser to four kings.

● Became a powerful man in Babylon.

Great experiences:

● Survived being thrown into a den of lions, when an angel shut the lions' mouths.

THE RULERS

Nebuchadnezzar

● Rich, proud and powerful king of the Babylonian Empire.

● Was troubled by a dream about a great statue until he asked Daniel for help.

● Years later, he made a huge golden statue, which Daniel and his friends refused to worship.

Belshazzar

● The last king of Babylon.

● Held a feast at which a mysterious hand wrote three words on the wall, which Daniel was able to explain: God was going to bring destruction on his kingdom.

Darius

● Promoted Daniel to be his chief adviser.

● Was tricked into issuing a decree forbidding prayer for thirty days, causing Daniel to be thrown into the lions' den for disobeying it.

When God saved Daniel from the lions, King Darius issued a decree that everyone in his empire should respect Daniel's God.

HIS FRIENDS

Hananiah, Mishael and Azariah

● Taken to Babylon, and educated for the king's service, they were renamed **Shadrach**, **Meshach** and **Abednego**.

● Refused to eat food used in idol worship.

● Refused to worship Nebuchadnezzar's golden statue, and were put into a blazing furnace.

● Survived the furnace unharmed, and were given great responsibility.

King Nebuchadnezzar expected everyone to worship his enormous golden statue. But Shadrach, Meshach and Abednego would only worship the one true God, the God of Israel.

Look it up

- *Daniel is taken to Babylon* DANIEL 1:1–21
- *The blazing furnace* DANIEL 3
- *The writing on the wall* DANIEL 5
- *The den of lions* DANIEL 6:1–24

Connections

1) Find three other people who, like Daniel, dealt with lions, on pages 11, 14 and 15.

2) Look for another Jewish exile who was given a position of power on page 20.

3) Turn to page 7 to find another man to whom God gave the power to interpret dreams.

BABYLON

The Jewish captives were taken to the wealthy city of Babylon. Archaeologists have found remains of city walls wide enough for chariots to drive on, and a massive city gate.

King Nebuchadnezzar ordered his slaves to build a series of gardens on the roof of his palace for his wife, known as 'the hanging gardens of Babylon'.

The Prophets

MESSENGERS FOR GOD

TWO KINGDOMS

After King Solomon died, his kingdom was split into two parts, Israel (the northern kingdom) and Judah (the southern kingdom). Most of the kings that followed were not good leaders, and God's people did not keep his laws, but worshipped idols and were selfish and cruel. Meanwhile, the great superpowers of Assyria, Egypt and then Babylon were making empires. First the people of Israel were taken away to serve foreign kings, and later the people of Judah were taken. The great city of Jerusalem was destroyed in 586 BCE.

Isaiah was in the Temple when God spoke to him. 'Who will be my messenger?' asked God. 'Here am I. Send me,' Isaiah replied.

NAME: ISAIAH

Where he lived:

- Jerusalem.

Family:

- Son of **Amoz**.
- Married with at least two sons, **Shear-Jashub** and **Maher-Shalal-Hash-Baz**.

Background:

- May have been part of the royal family.
- Had a vision of God in the year **King Uzziah** died.
- Began his prophecies in about 740 BCE.
- With Micah, his prophecies were concerned mainly with Judah and Jerusalem.

The prophets were sent to warn God's people: God hated to see rich people doing nothing to help the poor.

The message:

- Warned God's people that they would be judged for ignoring God and his laws.
- Told rich and powerful people to look after the poor and disadvantaged.
- Predicted that God would send the Messiah to save the world.

ISAIAH'S CONTEMPORARIES

Micah *of* Moresheth

- Like Isaiah, he was a prophet during the reigns of kings **Jotham**, **Ahaz** and the godly **Hezekiah**.
- He told the people of Judah that God wanted his people to be fair and forgiving, not proud and disobedient.

Hosea *son of* Beeri

- A prophet through six kings in twenty-five years in Israel: **Zechariah**, **Shallum**, **Pekahiah**, **Pekah**, **Hoshea** and **Menahem**. All but Hoshea and Menahem were murdered by their successors.
- God showed Hosea that he continued to love his people despite their disobedience, just as Hosea loved his unfaithful wife, **Gomer**.

Amos *of Tekoa*

- A prophet through the reigns of Uzziah, king of Judah, and **Jeroboam II**, king of Israel.
- A shepherd-farmer who warned God's people in Israel to share their wealth with the poor.
- Predicted the coming of the Assyrians.

OTHER PROPHETS

Joel *son of* Pethuel

- Reminds God's people that God is full of love, and willing to forgive everyone who is sorry.
- Looks forward to the giving of the Holy Spirit at Pentecost.

Ezekiel

- Son of a priest, he was captured and taken to Babylon where he was called by God to be a prophet.
- In Babylon he saw how idol worship made the people cruel and selfish, and he warned God's people in Judah to turn back to God.
- Saw that one day God would come like a Great Shepherd and bring all his people back to Jerusalem to worship him.

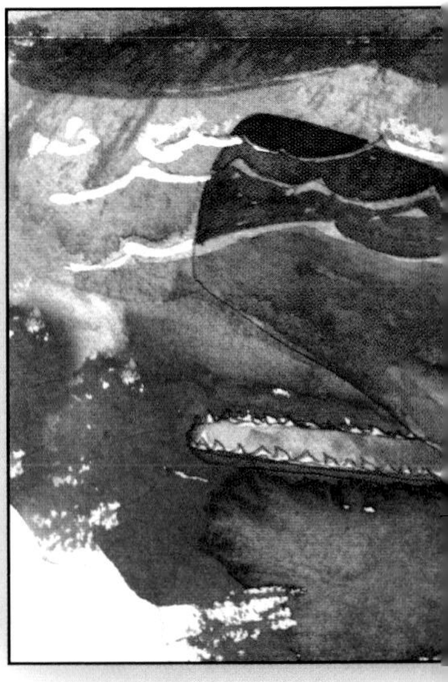

Jeremiah's prophecy was written down by Baruch the scribe.

Jonah *son of* Amittai

- Told by God to tell the people of Nineveh to stop doing evil things.
- Disobeyed God and ran away, until he was swallowed by a big fish.
- Gave the people the message and was angry that God forgave them when they were sorry and stopped their wrongdoing.

NAME: JEREMIAH

Where he lived:

- Jerusalem.

Family:

- Son of **Hilkiah**.
- God told him not to marry and have children because a time of great tragedy was coming.

Background:

- Son of a priest and a true follower of God.
- Started to speak out for God when young, and continued despite numerous attempts on his life.
- Lived through the reigns of the last five kings of Judah, **Josiah**, **Jehoahaz**, **Jehoiakim**, **Jehoiachin** and **Zedekiah**, before Jerusalem was destroyed by the Babylonians in 586 BCE.

His message:

- God wanted to be king of his people, and he had a plan for them.
- God hates idol worship, and people who know but do not obey his laws.
- Disaster would strike God's people and Jerusalem if they did not turn back to God.
- God would put things right in the end, forgiving his people and sending a new king for them, descended from King David.

Frustrations:

- The reluctance of the people to repent and obey God's laws.
- When he was thrown into a pit and left for dead for preaching God's message.

Disappointments:

- Often felt lonely and rejected by those around him. He was taken to Egypt after Jerusalem was conquered, and probably died there.

JEREMIAH'S SUPPORTERS

Ebed-Melech

- Ethiopian servant, who asked his master, King Zedekiah, to free Jeremiah from the pit.

Baruch

- Wrote down God's message to Jeremiah for King Jehoiakim.
- Read from Jeremiah's writings to the angry King Jehoiakim, who burnt the scroll.

Huldah

- A prophetess who told King Josiah that God would punish the people for their disobedience.

JEREMIAH'S CONTEMPORARIES

Nahum *of Elkosh*

- Writing at the time of King Josiah, he warned the people of Nineveh that God would judge them for their cruelty and wickedness.

Habakkuk *of Judah*

- Begged God to rescue his people from the Babylonians, and was told that God would judge all evil people one day.

Zephaniah

- Descendant of King Hezekiah.
- Warned God's people to turn away from worshipping idols and to ask for God's mercy.

Obadiah

- Warned that the enemy nation of Edom would suffer for their failure to help Judah after the fall of Jerusalem.

God sent a big fish to swallow the prophet Jonah to stop him running away from the task he had for him.

Look it up

- *Isaiah gets the message* ISAIAH 6:1–8
- *God speaks to Jeremiah* JEREMIAH 1:4–7
- *Jeremiah is thrown into a pit* JEREMIAH 38:1–13
- *The story of Jonah* JONAH 1–4

'You shall have no other god but me' was one of the commandments. But time after time, God's people ignored it. The prophets tried to warn people of the consequences of disobedience.

Connections

1) How does page 23 say that the prophet John the Baptist challenged people?

2) Look for someone on page 7 who, like Jeremiah, was thrown into a pit.

3) Find out which prophet challenged King David on page 15.

Esther THE WOMAN WHO SAVED HER PEOPLE

Look it up

- *The king chooses Esther*
  ESTHER 2:8–18
- *Haman's plot to destroy the Jews*
  ESTHER 3:8–15
- *Esther saves her people*
  ESTHER 7:1–6; 8:3–14

Connections

1) Turn to page 10 and read about two other women who saved their people.

2) Name four young men from page 17 who remained faithful to God when they were taken away into exile.

THE PERSIAN EMPIRE

The Persian Empire was so big that it covered the area between present-day Egypt and Turkey all the way east into present-day Iraq.

The book of Esther describes the luxury of the king's palace – purple wall hangings, silver decorations, marble pillars, and floors inlaid with jewels and semi-precious stones. At the king's banquet, wine was served in golden goblets.

Each year at the Jewish festival of Purim, the book of Esther is read and the people give thanks for her, remembering how she saved God's people.

Where she lived:

- Susa, capital of the Persian Empire.

Status:

- Member of the Jewish exiled community.

Occupation:

- Queen.

Childhood:

- Daughter of **Abihail**, she was orphaned as a child and brought up by her cousin, Mordecai.

Great experience:

- Was chosen to be wife of King Xerxes, ruler of Persia.

Most courageous action:

- Risked her life, by speaking up for her own people, the Jews.

HER FAMILY

Xerxes *husband*

- Fifth king of Persia, ruled from 486–465 BCE.
- Divorced **Queen Vashti** because she disobeyed him.
- Chose Esther above all the other beautiful women in the empire.

Before being chosen by the king, Esther had twelve months' beauty treatment.

Mordecai *cousin*

- Advised Esther and became a court official.
- Refused to worship Haman because it was against God's laws.
- Thwarted a plot to kill the king.
- Warned Esther of Haman's plot to destroy the Jews and asked her to use her position as queen to save them.

HER ENEMY

Haman

- King Xerxes' chief minister, he commanded everyone to bow down before him.
- Tricked Xerxes into issuing a decree to kill every Jew in the country in revenge against Mordecai.
- Was hanged on his own gallows after Esther let the king know of Haman's plans.

Esther pleaded with King Xerxes to save her people from certain death.

Esther replaced Vashti as queen and went to live in King Xerxes' winter palace in Susa.

Nehemiah THE MAN WHO PRAYED

Armed men stood guard while the city walls of Jerusalem were rebuilt.

Occupations:

- Royal cupbearer to **King Artaxerxes** of Persia.
- Later governor of Judah.

Where he lived:

- Persia and Jerusalem.

Status:

- An exiled member of the Jewish community living in Persia.
- Respected official in King Artaxerxes' court.

Personal qualities:

- Persistent and prayerful: when he heard that Jerusalem's walls were in ruins, he went without food and prayed for God's help.
- A good leader and organiser.

Major achievements:

- Led and completed the rebuilding of Jerusalem's damaged city walls.

Major sacrifices:

- Gave up a secure and comfortable job as a palace official in Persia to return to the ruins of Jerusalem, the home of his ancestors.

Frustrations:

- Opposition and ridicule from people who did not want him to complete the rebuilding work.

Great experiences:

- Saw the city walls restored and completed.
- Led a procession around the city walls thanking God for restoring Jerusalem.

HIS FAMILY

Hanani *brother*

- Came from Jerusalem to tell Nehemiah that the city walls were still in ruins.

OTHER LEADERS

Cyrus

- King of the Medes and Persians.
- Allowed the captive Jews to return to Jerusalem to rebuild the city and the Temple.
- Returned the Temple treasures captured by King Nebuchadnezzar.

Zerubbabel

- Son of **Shealtiel**.
- Led the first group of Jewish exiles from Babylon to rebuild the Temple nearly a hundred years before Nehemiah returned.

Haggai *and* Zechariah

- Prophets.
- Encouraged the returning exiles to rebuild the Temple.

Ezra *scribe*

- Spent his life studying God's laws: the history of God's people and how God wanted them to live.
- Taught these laws to the returning exiles in Jerusalem.
- Worked with Nehemiah.

Malachi *prophet*

- Urged people to worship God properly.

TROUBLEMAKERS

Sanballat

- Governor of Samaria who tried to stop the rebuilding work.

Tobiah

- A wealthy landowner who joined forces with Sanballat.

King Artaxerxes allowed Nehemiah to return to his homeland. He also provided the wood needed to rebuild the gates and walls of the city.

Look it up

- *Nehemiah and the king* NEHEMIAH 2:1–6
- *Nehemiah inspects the walls* NEHEMIAH 2:11–18
- *Ezra reads the Law* NEHEMIAH 8:1–18

Connections

1) Who, on page 17, tried to stop people praying for thirty days?

2) Look up page 15 to find out who first built the Temple in Jerusalem.

3) Find someone on page 9 who, like Sanballat and Tobiah, opposed her leader.

REBUILDING JERUSALEM

The Temple, the city walls and gates of Jerusalem had been destroyed by the Babylonians in 586 BCE following a long siege. Many of the Israelites were taken back to Babylon as slaves and captives.

When Nehemiah returned to Jerusalem more than one hundred years later, the Temple had been rebuilt but the walls lay in ruins. He encouraged the people not to give up – and the walls were rebuilt in fifty-two days.

Jesus God's Son, the perfect man

Joseph took Mary from Nazareth in Galilee to his hometown of Bethlehem in Judea, because he was descended from King David.

While Mary and Joseph were in Bethlehem, the time came for her baby to be born. She laid the baby Jesus in a manger, because there was no room in the inn.

Name:

- Jesus Christ. 'Christ' is the Greek form of Messiah, God's chosen one, the King who would reign for ever.

Place of birth:

- A stable, in Bethlehem in modern-day Israel.

Education:

- Learned to be a carpenter.
- Was taught the laws and history of the Jewish people at synagogue school.

Events at the time of his birth:

- **Caesar Augustus**, the ruler of the Roman Empire, ordered a census so that each man had to return to his family's home town.
- Angels told some shepherds that he had been born.
- When he was eight days old, his parents presented him in the temple in Jerusalem, where **Anna** and **Simeon**, servants of God, recognised him as God's Son, the promised Messiah.
- **Magi** or 'wise men' from the East who studied the stars saw signs in the sky that a new King had been born.

Childhood:

- Visited by Magi who brought him presents of gold, frankincense and myrrh.
- Escaped to Egypt with his parents when **King Herod the Great** ordered the execution of all boys in Bethlehem under two years old.
- Settled in Nazareth, where his parents lived.
- Was 'lost' in Jerusalem when he was twelve, and was found in the Temple.

What he said:

- God loves and cares for all people, and wants them to know him.
- Believing in him is the only way to become one of God's friends.
- Called God his Father, and told his friends to do the same.

What he did:

- Taught people about God and his kingdom, and how God wanted them to live.
- Controlled nature: stopped a storm on Lake Galilee, and walked on water.

Even before Jesus was born, Mary and Joseph knew he was a very special baby. An angel had told Mary that he would be called the Son of God.

- Befriended bad and unpopular people such as the tax collector, **Zacchaeus**.
- Made sick people well, such as **Bartimaeus** who was blind.
- Did some amazing things, such as feeding more than 5,000 people with five small loaves and two fishes.
- Brought the dead back to life, including his friend **Lazarus** and the daughter of **Jairus**, the leader of the synagogue.
- Lived a perfect life, doing nothing wrong.

Greatest struggles:

- Resisting the attempts of God's enemy, Satan, to tempt him to disobey God's plan.
- Against hypocrisy, as seen in the Pharisees and Sadducees, who said one thing and did another.
- Obeying God absolutely in the Garden of Gethsemane, even though it meant his death.

Saddest time:

- When he heard that Lazarus had died.

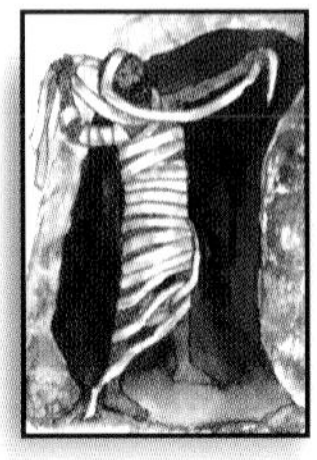

Lazarus had been dead for four days when Jesus called him from the tomb. He was still wrapped in his graveclothes.

People were shocked when a sinful woman poured expensive perfume over Jesus' feet. It was a sign of his coming death.

Unrepeatable achievements:

- Was resurrected or brought back to life by God after being executed on a cross and buried in a tomb.
- Returned to heaven, but sent the Holy Spirit to be active in the world throughout all time.

HIS FAMILY

Mary *mother*

- Told by the angel **Gabriel** that she was chosen by God to be the mother of Jesus.
- Eventually married Joseph.
- Stayed with Jesus when he was dying on the cross.

Joseph *Mary's husband*

- Was visited by an angel in a dream who told him about Mary's baby.
- Married Mary and brought Jesus up as his own son, teaching him the carpenter's trade.

Zechariah *uncle*

- Told by the angel Gabriel that he and his wife would have a son in their old age.
- Though a priest, he did not believe it possible, and was unable to speak until after the baby's birth.

Elizabeth *aunt*

- Gave birth to John, who became God's special messenger, preparing people for the coming of Jesus.

John the Baptist *cousin*

- Son of Elizabeth and Zechariah.
- His birth was foretold by the prophets of the Old Testament.
- Lived in the desert, wore clothes made of camels' hair, and ate wild honey.
- Challenged people to say sorry to God, and be baptised.
- Knew that Jesus was God's Son and baptised him in the River Jordan.
- Was beheaded by **King Herod Antipas** for criticising his marriage to **Herodias**.

THE EMPTY TOMB

Some people admire what Jesus said and did and say he was a good man. But what makes Jesus different from other good people?

Christians say that he was God. They say he really died and was buried, but that he rose again from the dead on the third day. When this happened, his friends were surprised; at first they could hardly believe it. His enemies were amazed; they tried to suggest the body had been stolen. But the body of the dead Jesus was never produced and the Bible tells us that hundreds of Jesus' followers saw Jesus, risen from the dead.

James, Jude, Simon, Joseph

- Jesus' brothers.
- Did not support Jesus at first.
- Later James and Jude became leaders of the church in Jerusalem and wrote letters to teach and encourage Christian believers.

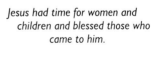

Jesus had time for women and children and blessed those who came to him.

Look it up

If you want to find out more about the life of Jesus, read one of the Gospels in a modern translation of the Bible. Mark's or Luke's Gospel is the best to start with.

- *The birth of Jesus* LUKE 2:1–16
- *Wise men visit the baby Jesus* MATTHEW 2:1–12
- *John the Baptist* MARK 1:1–8
- *Jesus calms a storm* MARK 4:35–41
- *Jesus feeds 5,000 people* JOHN 6:1–13
- *Jesus and Lazarus* JOHN 11:17–44
- *The Last Supper* MARK 14:12–26
- *Jesus put to death* MARK 15:1–47
- *Jesus is raised from death* MATTHEW 28:1–10

Connections

1) Turn to page 14 to find a famous king who spent his boyhood in Bethlehem.

2) Look for another king in another country who tried to put baby boys to death on page 9.

3) Find out how Jesus summed up the Ten Commandments on page 8.

4) Jesus learned to be a carpenter. Find out who learned to be a tentmaker on page 26.

5) Look for another prophet on page 16 who, like John, made a king and his wife angry.

Jesus' friends and enemies

Judas Iscariot, the disciple who betrayed Jesus, was in charge of the disciples' money.

CHRISTIANS

The first followers of Jesus Christ were called Christians. One of the last things Jesus told his followers to do was to tell other people about him, and to make them into 'disciples' or 'learners'.

Today there are millions of Christians all over the world, and translations of at least one book of the Bible have been made in over 2,000 languages.

JESUS' FRIENDS

The twelve disciples:

Peter, Andrew, James, John, Philip, Matthew, Thomas, Judas Iscariot, Simon the Zealot, Bartholomew, James (son of Alphaeus), Thaddaeus.

Profile:

- Chosen by Jesus to be with him in the three years he spent telling people about God's love.
- With him when he healed people or released them from evil spirits.
- Saw him have power over the natural world.
- Heard and remembered his teaching about the new life he came to bring.
- Saw him being put to death and witnessed his new life after his resurrection.
- Were ready to tell others the 'good news' of Jesus after he had returned to heaven.

Peter

- Son of **John**, brother of Andrew.
- A fisherman, called Simon until he became one of Jesus' three closest friends.
- When Jesus was arrested, Peter denied knowing him.
- Was filled with the Holy Spirit at Pentecost.
- Preached to a large crowd about Jesus, and many believed.
- Preached to a Gentile centurion called **Cornelius**, his family and friends, who all believed and were baptised.
- Was one of the leaders of the early church.

Andrew

- Son of John, brother of Peter.
- A fisherman who worked with Peter in Capernaum.
- Was one of John the Baptist's followers before he met Jesus.

James, *brother of John*

- A fisherman and one of Jesus' closest friends.
- One of the first Christians to die for his faith, James was killed by **Herod Agrippa I**.

John

- A fisherman and, with James, one of **Zebedee**'s sons.
- A very close friend of Jesus.

Matthew was a tax collector and was employed by the Romans occupying the country.

Peter wept bitterly when he realised he had betrayed his friend Jesus.

- Is thought to have written John's Gospel.

Philip

- A fisherman from Bethsaida.

Matthew

- Also known as Levi.
- A tax collector, who left his work to follow Jesus.

Thomas

- Doubted Jesus had been raised from death until he had seen him for himself.

Judas Iscariot

- Plotted with Jesus' enemies and betrayed him for thirty pieces of silver.
- Eventually killed himself.

Simon the Zealot

- So called either because he had been a rebel fighter or because he was really keen to follow Jesus.

Bartholomew

- Also known as Nathanael.

James *son of Alphaeus*

Thaddaeus

- Also known as **Judas**, son of **James**.

At least seven of Jesus' disciples were fishermen: Peter, Andrew, James, John, Philip, Thomas and Nathanael.

Martha served Jesus when he visited their home, while Mary sat at his feet and listened to him.

HIS FOLLOWERS

Mary, Martha and Lazarus

- Welcomed Jesus into their home.
- Jesus raised Lazarus from death.

Mary Magdalene

- Was healed by Jesus.
- Discovered his empty tomb, and met the risen Jesus.
- Told the disciples the tomb was empty.

Nicodemus

- Pharisee, Jewish council member.
- Came to talk to Jesus one night in secret, and later helped to bury Jesus' body.

Simon of Cyrene

- Carried Jesus' cross.

Joanna

- Supported Jesus with her own money.

Joseph of Arimathea

- Jewish council member.
- Asked Pilate if he could bury Jesus' body in the tomb he had bought for himself.

Cleopas

- Met the risen Jesus while walking home to Emmaus with a friend, but did not recognise him until Jesus started to eat a meal with them.

People Jesus met

- Jesus' mission was to show God's love to everyone, particularly the 'outcasts' of society. Many of the people he met are not named in the Bible. Here are some of them.

Everywhere Jesus went, people called out to him to be healed.

Jesus healed:

- ten men suffering from leprosy
- a paralysed man
- the servant of a Roman centurion
- a woman who had an incurable disease which made her an outcast.

Jesus showed God's love to:

- a rich young man
- the woman at the well
- babies and little children
- the thief who was crucified beside him.

The religious authorities did not approve of the things Jesus did and said. They plotted to get rid of him.

HIS ENEMIES

Annas

- Son of **Seth**.
- Jewish high priest from CE 6 to 15.
- Questioned Jesus to see whether he was guilty of blasphemy, before handing him over to Caiaphas.

Caiaphas

- Jewish high priest from CE 18 to 36 and at the trial of Jesus.
- Son-in-law of Annas.
- Leader of the Jewish council.
- Questioned Jesus and handed him over to Pilate.

Pilate, the Roman governor, did not know what to do with Jesus but gave in to the crowd who wanted him crucified.

Pontius Pilate

- Roman governor.
- Responsible for the province of Judea.
- Knew that Jesus was innocent of the charges made by the Jewish authorities, but gave in to pressure to have Jesus crucified.

Barabbas

- Jewish terrorist.
- Murderer and freedom fighter, chosen by the crowd to be released from the death sentence instead of Jesus.

Look it up

- *Jesus calls the first disciples* MATTHEW 4:18–22
- *Jesus heals many people* MATTHEW 8:14–17
- *Jesus and the tax collector* MATTHEW 9:9–13
- *Jesus chooses the twelve disciples* MARK 3:13–19
- *Judas betrays Jesus* MARK 14:10–11
- *Peter denies Jesus* MARK 14:66–72
- *The empty tomb* JOHN 20:1–18
- *Jesus appears to his disciples* JOHN 20:19–29
- *The coming of the Holy Spirit* ACTS 2:1–6

Connections

1) Jesus made friends with all sorts of unlikely people. Can you find on this page a Pharisee who was his friend, and on page 26 another Pharisee who became a great Christian?

2) The disciples were ordinary men who left everything to become disciples of Jesus. Which prophet on page 16 left his family to serve God?

3) Find a disciple who was a tax collector on page 24, and another tax collector who followed Jesus on page 22.

4) Look at page 18 to see which prophet looked forward to Jesus sending his Holy Spirit on the Day of Pentecost.

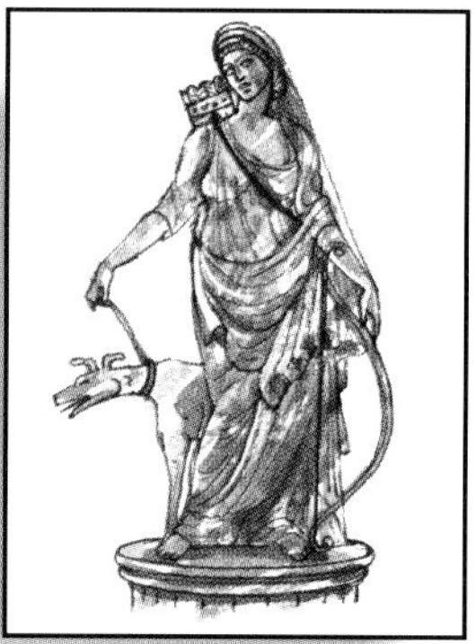

Diana the huntress, also known as Artemis, was a very popular Greek goddess.

Paul A MAN WITH A MISSION

Name:
● Called by the Jewish name of Saul until he met Jesus, when the Roman name Paul is used.

Education:
● Well-educated, he studied Jewish law with **Gamaliel**, one of the top teachers.

● Learned the skill of tentmaking.

Background:
● A Pharisee from the Jewish tribe of Benjamin, but born in Tarsus in Cilicia (now Turkey) and a Roman citizen.

Occupations:
● Tentmaker.

● Later a leader and teacher in the early church.

Mistakes:
● Persecuted and killed many Christians because he thought they were wrong.

● Approved when **Stephen**, one of the leading preachers and miracle-workers among the early Christians, was stoned to death.

Greatest experience:
● Met the risen Jesus on the road to Damascus, and became a Christian believer.

Bad experiences:
● Received death threats for telling people about Jesus.

● Was beaten and frequently put in prison.

● Was saved from shipwreck on his way to Rome for trial.

Great achievements:
● Made three long and difficult journeys through the Roman Empire, to present-day Turkey, Greece and Cyprus, telling people about Jesus.

● Even when he was chained up he wrote letters to the Christians in the places he had visited and some of these have become part of the New Testament.

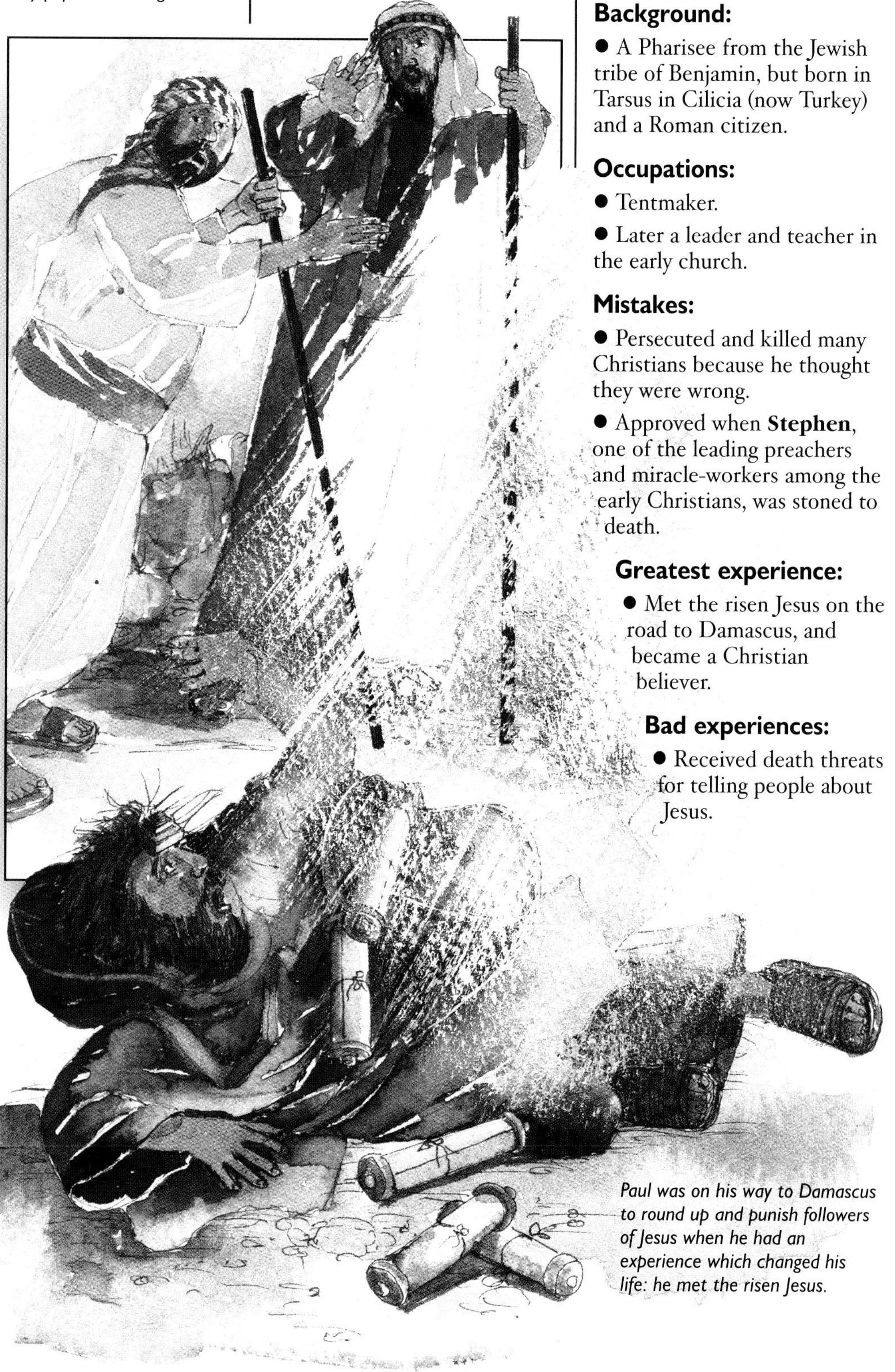

Paul was on his way to Damascus to round up and punish followers of Jesus when he had an experience which changed his life: he met the risen Jesus.

HIS SPECIAL FRIENDS

Aquila and Priscilla
● Tentmakers who worked with Paul, telling people about Jesus.

Barnabas
● Sold his possessions to share with the other Christians in Jerusalem.

● Supported Paul when he first became a Christian and worked closely with him.

Silas
● A Roman citizen, he lived in Jerusalem, and went with Paul on one of his journeys.

● Was with Paul when an earthquake broke their prison chains, and the Philippian jailer and his family became Christians.

Timothy
● Son of **Eunice** and grandson of **Lois**.

● Went with Paul on his second and third journeys and received two letters from him.

Paul travelled hundreds of miles to tell people about Jesus.

HIS SUPPORTERS

Ananias
- Told Paul what Jesus wanted him to do and befriended him.

Apollos
- Was taught about the Holy Spirit by Aquila and Priscilla.
- Became an excellent preacher and teacher.

Archippus
- A 'fellow soldier' in God's work.

Aristarchus
- A Macedonian who often went with Paul on his journeys.

Demas
- With Paul when he was first in prison, but deserted Paul during his second imprisonment.

Epaphras
- Founder of the church at Colossae, and visited Paul in prison in Rome.

Epaphroditus
- Sent to look after Paul while in prison.

Erastus
- Sent by Paul to Macedonia with Timothy.

Eutychus
- Became sleepy while Paul was preaching at night and died when he fell out of a window. Paul brought him back to life.

John Mark
- Nephew of Barnabas, he probably wrote the Gospel of Mark.
- Went with Paul and Barnabas on their first missionary journey.

Luke
- A doctor who went with Paul on his journeys and helped him when he was ill.
- Is thought to have written the Gospel of Luke and the book of Acts.

Lydia
- A rich trader in purple cloth, she became a believer in Jesus in Philippi and gave food and shelter to Paul and his companions.

Lydia and her friends were by the river outside Philippi when they heard the 'good news' about Jesus.

Onesimus
- Runaway slave who became a believer and Paul's trusted helper until he was returned to his Christian master, **Philemon**.

Titus
- Collected money for the church in Jerusalem.
- Received a letter from Paul to help him in his work with the Christians in Crete.

Tychicus
- Tychicus went with Paul from Ephesus to give money to the church in Jerusalem.
- Was also sent with Paul's letters to the churches at Colossae and Ephesus.

HIS ENEMIES

Ananias
- The high priest who questioned Paul when he was brought before him as president of the Sanhedrin, the Jewish council.

King Aretas
- Ruler of Damascus, he tried to arrest Paul who escaped by being lowered from the city walls in a basket.

Demetrius
- A silversmith in Ephesus, he made statues of the Greek goddess, Artemis.
- Stirred up others to riot when Paul preached that there was no God other than Jesus.

Felix
- Roman governor of Judea, he put Paul in prison to please the Jewish leaders and because he hoped to receive money for releasing him.

Festus
- Succeeded Felix as governor of Judea.
- Convinced that Paul was innocent, but agreed he should go to Rome for trial so that he didn't offend Paul's enemies. **King Herod Agrippa II**, who was visiting, also heard Paul's case and agreed with Festus.

Tertullus
- A lawyer who accused Paul of being a troublemaker.

Look it up

Paul meets Jesus on the road to Damascus ACTS 9:1–19

Paul is shipwrecked ACTS 27:13–44

Connections

1) Find four people on page 22 whose lives, like Paul's, were changed when they met Jesus.

2) Look for another man with a message from God who had a bad experience at sea on page 19.

PAUL THE SURVIVOR

Paul and his companions travelled hundreds of miles by land and sea, spreading the 'good news' about Jesus. He was often beaten up and imprisoned, and survived terrible shipwrecks, but nothing would stop him.

Paul wrote many encouraging letters to Christians while under house arrest in Rome. These letters are now part of the New Testament.

Paul suffered his fourth shipwreck while travelling to Rome to stand trial. The ship with 276 crew and passengers broke up off the coast of Malta, but all reached land safely.

Index

The order of each entry is as follows: person, page number, Bible reference.

Answers to Connections

PAGE 4
1. Joseph's brothers planned to murder him.
2. God promised that Abraham's descendants would be a great nation.

PAGE 5
1. Elizabeth and Zechariah.
2. Egypt and Babylon.
3. Mary and Joseph.

PAGE 7
1. Aaron.
2. Under the leadership of Joshua.
3. Joseph was Jesus' earthly father, and Simeon recognised that he was the Messiah.
4. Abram to Abraham, Simon to Peter and Saul to Paul.

PAGE 9
1. It was called that because of God's promise to Abraham.
2. They were all descendants from Jacob, Joseph and his brothers.
3. Elijah.
4. They did not support Jesus at first. Then some believed in him.
5. David.

PAGE 11
1. David.
2. Ruth.
3. Esther.
4. Judas Iscariot.

PAGE 12
1. David.
2. Sarah, Rachel, Manaoh's wife and Elizabeth.
3. Aaron.

PAGE 13
1. By a stone from David's sling.
2. Jesus was the new king, descended from King David.
3. Paul.

PAGE 15
1. Samson.
2. Eli.
3. It was destroyed.

PAGE 16
1. Enoch.
2. The Ten Commandments.
3. Jeremiah, Zephaniah and Ezekiel.

PAGE 17
1. Samson, David and Benaiah.
2. Esther.
3. Joseph.

PAGE 19
1. To say sorry to God and be baptised.
2. Joseph.
3. Nathan.

PAGE 20
1. Deborah and Jael.
2. Shadrach, Meshach, Abednego and Daniel.

PAGE 21
1. Darius.
2. Solomon.
3. Miriam.

PAGE 23
1. David.
2. The Pharaoh, king of Egypt.
3. Love God with all your heart, mind and strength, and treat others as you would like them to treat you.
4. Paul.
5. Elijah.

PAGE 25
1. Nicodemus and Paul.
2. Elisha.
3. Matthew and Zacchaeus.
4. Joel.

PAGE 27
1. Zacchaeus, Lazarus, Jairus' daughter and Bartimaeus.
2. Jonah.

Little EAGLE

Published in the UK by Eagle Publishing
PO Box 530, Guildford, Surrey GU2 4FH

ISBN 0 86347 437 3

First edition 2001

British Library Cataloguing in Publication Data.
A catalogue record for this book is available from the British Library.

Printed and bound in Malaysia